How to Heal

From Fear of

Abandonment

How to Heal From Fear of Abandonment

By

Nancy Sungyun

How to Heal From Fear of Abandonment

By Nancy Sungyun

Copyright © 2020 by Nancy Sungyun

Published and distributed in the United States.

Printed in the United States of America

Copyright page

Dedication

This book is dedicated to all who have suffered the fear of abandonment and are now ready to be free.

Table of content

How to Heal From Fear of Abandonment

Introduction

Fear of abandonment often goes undetected or is not paid enough attention. The victim of this fear too often attaches to themselves identities, the very symptoms of the fear, living in shame and low self-esteem which burrows them further and deeper into the pit of this fear.

When you have fear of abandonment, you react to situations and relationships in ways that can make you feel as if you are weak, petty, unevolved, shallow, jealous, etc. When, in truth, you are experiencing excruciating pain that feels almost like death itself sometimes. The fact is that you had gained the fear because something real actually happened to you (likely during your childhood) and you were brought to believe that you would and could be abandoned and experience the terrible feeling that you once felt when you had no power to help yourself.

You are not petty or weak. You just have to heal the part of you that i injured, that is all.

The last thing that you need is to give yourself grief because you are reacting to unresolved pain.

If you had a physical injury, that area of your body is going to need tending to: time and care to heal. If someone comes near it you would react with pain and everyone would understand that you have an injury.

Oftentimes, fear of abandonment is undetectable. Most people do not know that you have an injury to tend to and heal. In fact, you may have even forgotten that you have an injury to heal. So, when you react to painful events (touch to an injured part), everyone around you may think you are overreacting. You likely also are thinking that you are overreacting. And then, of course, you feel bad about yourself. You are putting metaphorical salt on your own wounds. Actually, you are putting germs on your open cut. You will learn more about that later in this book.

What you have to do is tend to the emotional injury that caused you to have this fear of abandonment.

I too used to let my fear of abandonment rule my life in more ways than one. I only watched the symptoms of it and felt bad about myself. I never really attended to the source of the problems that were occurring in my life because of it.

My fear of abandonment truly cost me a lot: relationships, career success, and, fundamentally, the quality of my life.

If you have fear of abandonment, it is crucial that you conquer it so that you can live a life free of the negative manifestations that it creates and be free to experience the joy of life.

...

One of the greatest discoveries a man makes,
one of his great surprises, is to find he can do
what he was afraid he couldn't do.

—Henry Ford

Chapter 1 - How I came to have a fear of abandonment

I lost my mom and the rest of my biological family when I was three years old.

I was given to a mom, a woman who could not conceive and was deathly afraid that her husband would leave her because of that.

My first mom, my biological mom, was selling *banchan*, which translates as, "side dishes" at the outdoor marketplace to support me and her when she met my second mom's older sister, Yebin.

My first mom could always count on seeing Yebin with her little girl, just about 6 months older than me holding a selling spot right next to her. Yebin sold roasted sweet potatoes and roasted chestnuts during the winter.

Poverty was stiflingly ubiquitous during those days in South Korea, a then third world country. Suffering was the norm. But then again, Korea had become accustomed to suffering for some time, the neighbor's occupation, then war: the very reasons for the extreme poverty of those days.

It would be Yebin, who would broker the meeting between her wealthy younger sister, my future second mom, and my poverty-stricken young single mom who was struggling to feed and shelter her and me.

~

My biological mom wrote up a contract that she signed in which she declared that if my new mom had a change of heart about me, she was to give me back to her and no one else.

In my forties, I would find out about the contract that was signed between them. I also learned that my adoptive mom threw the contract into the fire pit.

~

I do not remember what I felt that day when I was taken away from my first mom by Yebin. I do know what grew and rooted deep in my heart and being, which was that I must not be wantable, likable, and lovable. I wasn't important. A person whom I love could walk away, leave me behind, and forget about me as if I had never existed.

This would become my fear of abandonment. Upon that seed of fear, I would then be taught how scary my life would become upon being abandoned by the sheer amount of fear and pain that my adoptive parents would provide for me.

On top of being left behind, I learned that being left behind meant a life of fear that I could hardly bear.

~

My new mom went fast to work, using her wealth to bribe the government officials to change my place of birth, a new name, and date of birth. I can only guess that she did this to make sure my first mom could not find me in the future. The date of my birth served that purpose and also another. She would make me about six months older so that I could enter 1st grade at the same time as that little girl that I used to see at the market.

No, this was not so that that little girl and I could see each other in school, so that I could have a friend. We lived in very different neighborhoods and would go to very different schools.

My second mom wanted me to beat my new cousin in achievements that she thought would give her some points in the family. It would be a disappointing attempt on her part since I would become a very mediocre if not a bad student in school, while my little cousin would leave me in the dust by excelling in every subject and even in art.

I would be a disappointment to her in every way except in two ways. I was physically strong and healthy. She could feel little concern about beating me to run her frustrations through and could have me take over the housework, cooking, cleaning, and washing clothes and bedding when she and her husband would later become poorer and poorer and could no longer pay to keep the house staff.

~

They would go on for the next 13 years of my life, powerfully reinforcing the notion that I was not worthy of love and giving me reasons for why my first mom left me. I was bad and I was unlovable and, to make matters even worse, I was ugly and far from feminine.

My second mom would tell me that if I had been girlier, my father, her husband, would not want to beat me as he did.

~

They were controlling while being neglectful. It may sound contradictory but it happened in the following ways. They were extremely cold, unloving, and never looked at me with feelings of love or affection. They were either indifferent or repugnant.

Of course, they never said anything nice to me, never mind "I love you", but there was never a feeling that I was important to them in any way. They never made sure I ate, if anything they hid foods that they liked from me so that I would not eat them.

They also repeatedly told me that I didn't have the right look. I was ugly. I was loud. I acted like a boy, not a girl. They treated me in general as unworthy of not only love but just about anything good.

I had no worth to them unless I was doing things for them.

In that toxic environment, I learned to fear life and reject myself.

The constant jokes at the expense of my looks, my voice, my walk, everything that a normal child my age would do added to my feeling of being unwantable.

I was constantly not allowed to do things that normal kids were allowed to do like play with toys at other people's homes. While other kids could, my adoptive father would give me a look that said, "Don't you dare touch those things, you don't deserve them." All of these things would of course go on to cement the belief that my being left by my mom made sense.

~

The feelings, beliefs, and paradigm that I adopted reinforced my toxic beliefs about myself, my world, and the conditions of my life. This then then strengthened my belief that I was worthless and would inevitably lead a loveless, lonely life.

The way I carried on my life with those beliefs, not being aware of how those feelings were affecting me, but being affected still the same kept me in a cycle of negative and harmful events. Those events only reaffirmed the very fear of abandonment that clung to me like a very stubborn barnacle.

Living with a fear of abandonment was my life companion that I did not detect. When the symptoms would appear I would experience shame and low self-esteem for having those symptoms, defining myself based on those symptoms, and becoming even more afraid of abandonment every day.

I treated myself harshly, lacking understanding, lacking self-belief, and lacking self-compassion all while giving myself abundant and constant insults.

I saw the world through the lens of fear and defensiveness. Everyone was always about to do something wrong to me. I had a hard time trusting anyone to truly care about me, yet I desperately wanted to trust someone to care about me. So, I swung from one extreme to the next: being gullible at the sight of imagined love and then running at the worst time from someone who could have honestly loved me.

I had a heart full of ambition to find a way to be lovable at last, to find a way to have reasons for people to love me and never leave me. My method was trying to become extraordinarily lovable, needable, valuable, meaningful, and important to people. My ambitions made my failures even more painful.

~

I failed at a singing career at age four because I could not pronounce a sound correctly for recordings and began my career of failures.

I failed again at a singing career when I was in 4th grade. I hiked up the hill in downtown Seoul to a TV station where they held something that would today be like the American Idol but was held weekly and they filmed the tryouts live.

I went there every Thursday for the whole school year and every Thursday when my turn was up, I would turn around and come back home without trying out. That was about over an hour each way, two buses, then the hike up, then down the hill.

I quit or didn't complete many more things in my life in almost the exact same fashion as when I was in 4th grade. I gave up on myself regarding too many things to mention or even remember.

I never gave my all to anything. I never could cross that threshold as I judged myself to be undeserving of anything that good. After all, I was not good and I was not worthy of love or anything else good.

It didn't matter how many people came along and tried to show me that I had something special to offer. Their words would hit my disbelief and bounce off me just as fast as they came.

~

I saw the world through the lens of someone who was going to lose if there was a battle of any kind.

I saw the world through the lens of someone who was always going to be used but not appreciated, may be needed but never loved.

I believed that I was always to be rejected.

So desperate for love, yet feeling doomed for failure at getting love or anything like the success that I wanted in life, I only went deeper into my fear of abandonment.

~

I always believed that there was something innately unlikeable about me. I believed if anyone liked me that I had fooled them and they would eventually find out that I was dislikable.

I lived that out and made my fear come true by letting friendships and other important relationships go if I feared they were over.

I was always ready to feel injured so if someone said something or did something that may or may not have been on purpose, I would be offended and would act on it based on those feelings. Of course, then what I feared would happen. Alternatively, I would assume what I feared would happen and I would create the outcome that matched what I feared was true. I would make the relationships end fearing they were going to end anyway. I fell deep into the victim mindset.

~

The victim mindset and other negative and destructive beliefs that I had deepened my fear. I carried the victim mindset inside me for many decades. My victim mindset helped to perpetuate my victim mindset.

And what I created, manifested by my reactions to my life's events, the very reactions caused by my victim mindset, produced more fear of abandonment. And the fear became even deeper.

It is a terrible catch 22. You have a fear of abandonment, thus you continue to have fear of abandonment. It has to stop somewhere, right?

...

Your visions will become clear only
when you can look into your own heart.
Who looks outside, dreams; who looks
inside, awakes.

— *C.G. Jung*

Chapter 2 - The signs that you have a fear of abandonment

The problem with having a fear of abandonment is that many people often do not link the symptom of the fear to the right culprit. What I mean by this is that when you have a fear of abandonment, you react, acting, and making decisions based on a fear of abandonment while not knowing that you are doing that.

For too many people and too often, the reactions that you have become a source of embarrassment, shame, and harsh self-talk that only leaves you deeper in this fear of abandonment.

What makes this even worse is that others around you do not understand what is going on with you and they too react negatively to your symptoms.

What most people then do is try and stop the symptoms. They feel desperate to stop the symptoms only to either drown out and disconnect from the true feelings or fail to stifle the symptoms over and over again. It makes you feel weak and a failure at life.

In this chapter, I want to go over with you the many symptoms that manifest because of a fear of abandonment. That way, you can see for yourself that your common reactions to them are there not because you are weak or something is terribly wrong with you, but just because you need to heal what is ailing you.

~

When you blame yourself or put yourself down or feel ashamed of the feelings and emotions that you experience from a fear of abandonment, it is like blaming yourself for having a headache, runny nose, fever, chills, inability to work, unable to eat, etc., because you have the flu. All those symptoms are there because you have to heal from the flu.

All of your negative feelings and reactions are there because you have to heal the fear of abandonment.

~

So, let's take a look at the symptoms in your life, that are screaming and crying out to let you know that you have a fear of abandonment and you need to heal so that you can be free to be as happy and self-confident as you truly deserve to be.

~

You constantly worry that someone will dislike you or disapprove of you.

If you find yourself worrying about what you said, what you did, how you said, what you said, and fear that whoever you interacted with may dislike you, judge you, look down on you, disrespect you, think ill of you, talk about you in a negative way… All of these are signs that you are afraid of getting rejected by people, and you probably have a fear of abandonment. You fear that, by being abandoned by these people, you will mean nothing: you will be a meaningless nothing. If you feel this way often, then you most likely have a deep fear of abandonment.

If you second-guess things that you said, things that you did, things that you decided on because you are worried that someone will be disappointed with you, judge you wrong, or decide that you are not right for them, you are fearing rejection. That fear comes from fearing abandonment.

You worry so much about being disliked or disapproved of that your mind is preoccupied with those thoughts.

You see your mind doing this, you see yourself feeling this and you might even feel like something is wrong with you.

You really do not often have a rest from self-questioning and self-judging. You are constantly worrying about every aspect of you. I this is your normal, you likely have a deep fear of abandonment.

~

You constantly worry that people who you love will leave you or reject you or that something could happen to them and you might lose them.

You fear anyone that you love could leave you, judge you, dislike you, forget about you, think of you as meaningless, not important, that they do not genuinely love you.

And, if you think that they love you, you then fear you may lose them in other ways. You fear danger for them in some way. You fear you may cause that by doing innocent random things.

You have the irrational fear that if you do something that is completely unrelated that you might cause them harm. You become fearful of making innocent, simple, and unrelated decisions because you don't want to cause anyone that you love to be harmed in any way.

You are overprotective and even controlling of your loved ones, lovers, your children, any of your family members, friends, anyone that is important to you. You do everything that you can to protect them from harm, or perceived threats of harm.

You might find yourself feeling jealous and inadequate, not worthy of the person that you love, and fear that they will find someone better than you.

When you feel jealous, your fear is so overwhelming and you become utterly overwhelmed with fear and pain that you don't know what to do. You either act out or retreat feeling ashamed of your jealous feelings and your low self-esteem. You feel worthless.

If you have a loving partner you feel bad for going through an episode of jealousy and fear.

If you have a less than a loving partner, especially one that might be lacking empathy or even a narcissist, that partner will use how you behaved against you and make you feel even worse than you already do. And it is likely that they did things to cause you to feel insecure and jealous in the first place, but you with your low self-esteem will just go with what they say about you.

If you have the tendency to feel insecure and your partner is narcissistic, they will enjoy making you feel bad and then blaming you for feeling bad. You in fear of losing their love will not see anything that they have done, you will just sit there fearing that you did something wrong and that you might be abandoned.

If someone likes you, you believe it is because they have been fooled and eventually they will find out who you truly are and instantly dislike you.

You have a general belief that if someone likes you it is because they don't know the real you. They've been fooled. You fooled them. You have been pretending and being likable but, soon, you will not be able to help but to let your mask drop.

You think that they will eventually find out who you really are and then they will despise you because you are, deep inside, really that bad and unlikable.

Everything that you do is under scrutiny for you, your own scrutiny that is. You remember how you smiled. You remember how you coughed wrong. You remember how you opened the door too late for that person that you were trying to meet. You remember how you may have missed something that someone said and may have replied wrong so, on and on.

It seems that you are always doing something wrong and you are constantly terrified that someone will notice.

You imagine that you will be found out for the big ball of mess that you are. All the incessant worries in your heart do not help in terms of making you feel better about yourself, of course.

You incessantly worry about the actions that you take, second-guessing all the time, worrying that you might disappoint someone or cause someone to dislike.

You constantly worry about doing something wrong. You fear that you might make a mistake or fail, or do something in a way that others do not approve of. You worry about what you did or what you produced or what you made with fear. You worry that you did a terrible job or you made the wrong thing or you made it wrong. You worry about your work and think you will be rejected.

You never feel good enough about the things that you work on, create, or produce. You don't think anything you do is ever good enough, no matter what other people might say.

~

You constantly second guess your decisions.

You are afraid that your decisions may cause people that you care about and feel close to — that you want in your life— to abandon you. So, you have a hard time making decisions about things that you want to do with your life. You have come to distrust your ability to make decisions that keep you safe from being abandoned so you fear making many or any decisions at all.

Every decision, from small to large decisions, makes you feel apprehensive. Feeling apprehensive makes you feel even worse and less worthy of being liked, so your fear of being left, rejected, and abandoned continues.

You fear even deciding what you eat, wear, or do for fun, for fear of being judged wrong and being disliked or rejected, so you wait for others to decide for you. You, in fact, like what others like better than what you like. You even feel unsure about what you like, thinking that your opinions, thoughts, and feelings are inferior. You feel safest when someone else's opinions is apparent and you follow someone else's advice ahead of yours. You look indecisive and unable to make up your mind. When you see the frustration in others' faces, you feel rejection and disapproval. You feel terrible about your weakness and your inability to make up your mind. You even feel bad about the fact that you don't know what you like, what you want, and what is most important to you. This reinforces your feelings of unimportance and worthlessness. You feel like nothing because of this condition, continuing to make you live in fear.

You continue to worry about making the wrong decisions.

To make matters worse for you, people in your life often lose patience with you because it takes you so long to make up your mind about things. It might be deciding to go somewhere. It might be deciding what to make for dinner. It might be deciding what to choose on the menu. It might be deciding what to wear to a party. It might be deciding what life path to follow... big or small, you worry about the consequences of your decisions. You never give yourself the right to make a choice that is purely based on what you want. You do not want to be rejected, no matter the cost.

~

You often worry that others are judging you

You constantly look over your shoulder to make sure you are not being judged by others.

You're often afraid that others are judging, and judging you in a negative light. You are afraid that they are thinking of all the ways that make you look bad, not smart enough, not good enough or not attractive enough or not hardworking enough, not likable enough, don't listen enough, did not do enough, did not shine enough... everything about you is not enough.

~

You do not feel good about yourself.

Your fear of abandonment leads to a constant mode of critiquing everything about you based on your guesses as to what you think others want from you so that you are not rejected and abandoned. It makes it very difficult and almost impossible to feel any kind of good feeling about yourself genuinely and consistently. If you ever do feel good about yourself it is fleeting and dependent on the positive responses that you receive from someone.

Nothing that you do can be good enough since you will find imperfections in any and all things that you do and have done. You think that possibly the only way to be completely immune to rejection and being abandoned is by being perfect in every way. And that, of course, is a lose-lose solution since no one, including you, is ever perfect in every way.

~

You have a hard time spending time by yourself.

You are afraid to be alone because being alone is to you evidence of you not being worthy of love. When you are alone, you feel empty and meaningless, and that feels too painful or too scary. You do everything that you can to avoid feeling those things.

You do everything that you can to avoid being alone. You beg, negotiate, and even compromise your sense of pride to be with others and not be alone.

When you are alone you feel like a loser or a failure. When you are alone you feel like no one. When you are alone you feel like you have no worth. You actively arrange your life so that you are surrounded by people. You do anything and everything to avoid being alone and when you are you feel depressed.

~

You feel alone even when you are surrounded by others.

You have a hard time believing that anyone truly likes, loves, or cares about you so even when you're surrounded by all those love you're not certain of, it only reminds you that you might just be unlovable or unworthy of love. Your fear reinforces that you really deserve to be rejected and abandoned.

Even if they love you, you cannot really see it or feel it. You can easily feel rejected because you are in constant fear of being rejected. If someone makes a face thinking of something completely unrelated to you, you may internalize it and think they don't like you so you assume that you have been rejected.

You feel a general sense of not belonging anywhere. You feel that no one really and truly knows you or understands you.

You feel like everyone else is connecting with each other but not you.

~

You do things to get love.

You find yourself doing things that you do not really want to do because they might result in you getting approval or feeling liked or loved. You almost always feel pressure to do things that you do not want to do.

You might over-promise to pull people in. You might talk a lot about things that you want to do for them so that they like you and want you without really being able to do what it is that you promised to produce or give them.

Your impulse is to make them happy first, but this ends up causing you stress and trouble later when you have to follow through with the promises that you have made.

You find yourself going out of your way to do things for people, even if they do nothing for you in return. You might find yourself constantly thinking about what they need, how you can help them, and do things to make them happy even if they never ever do anything for you to make you feel happy or take care of you to make you feel special. You might feel unhappy yet still compelled to do things for those people.

~

You have a hard time saying no and making what you want a priority.

You have a very difficult time saying no, even if you really need to say no and want to say no.

You end up giving much more of everything than you can or should. You end up sacrificing your own life to make someone else happy, which almost always leaves you feeling empty. You can often feel used because many humans do not know how to not go along with it. You often feel unloved and unappreciated because people just get used to all the things that you do and perhaps they even want more or ask for more and you feel awful.

You have a hard time saying no to things that you cannot afford the time to do but you find yourself figuring out how to do it at the expense of your well-being and sense of peace.

You feel compelled and obligated to do everything that people close to you ask or need.

Saying no is one of the most difficult things for you to say. Saying no to: time spent, money given, attention given, activities that you are not interested in, things that your heart is not in, or people that you do not necessarily want to spend time with. The hardest one to say no to is to people who are close to you. Even if they are being unreasonable and uncaring toward you when they ask for what they want, you still have a hard time saying no to them.

~

You give too much in relationships.

You always end up giving much more than you receive because you feel as if you have to earn your worth. You don't always know how people in your life actually feel. You don't really know if they love you for you or for what you do for them. You would rather not be rejected or abandoned than find out if they do not value you. So, you do everything for them to make sure that you will always be needed.

You become the do-gooder, the supporter, the ever-loyal partner, or friend. You give so much that you leave yourself very little left to carry out your own life in the way that you need or want.

This often makes others take you for granted and some even use you. When you are taken for granted you feel hurt and abandoned so what do you do then? You do more to see if you can pull them back to love you, to not leave you. Whenever you do things for them, you get the momentary good reaction out of them, which quickly fades. This then forces you to think quickly of more to do for them to get that jolt of brief happiness from the positive reaction that you get from that person. This becomes a vicious and self-sabotaging cycle.

~

You have a hard time trusting others.

It is difficult for you to trust others since you know that they are going to abandon you. You want to belong so much that you will get close to people but you will struggle with the closeness. You will push and pull and you will constantly question their feelings for you thinking that their feelings will likely soon go away.

If even the person loves you, it is hard for you to trust that their love will stay, which causes you to be suspicious, jealous, controlling, and possessive. Often the other people fall away only to affirm your suspicion that everyone goes away. You believe once again that everyone abandons you.

~

You push people away before getting rejected.

You might push people away before they can abandon you so that you don't have to experience getting hurt. You may never really allow people to get close to you. You might even just keep all relationships distant and, when it comes to intimate relationships, you might just keep away or find excuses to leave the relationship before you have to find out that they will eventually leave you anyway.

~

You feel very insecure in romantic relationships, friendships, and all relationships

You are always busy looking for ways that you might be rejected which puts you in a position of looking for ways to get people's approval instead of seeing if you even really like them.

This can land you in relationships that are far less than what you want and need.

You put your value beneath the value of the others as you keep aiming to please them, to be loved and accepted by them, not to be rejected by them, never really looking to truly and deeply learn their value.

You can never really enjoy being loved or liked.

If they like or love you a lot you think that there is something wrong with them.

If they don't like or love you enough, that is the right temperature and you are comfortable in knowing that you have to earn their love.

If they give you love you look for all the flaws in them so that you can have reasons to leave them.

~

You feel codependent

Your feelings are affected by others around you because you are focused on gauging what they are feeling so that you do not get rejected. You become very dependent on them for all your emotional needs, and you become very involved in taking care of their wants and needs.

~

You often feel needy and clingy

You feel like you need those who you care about to be around you all the time to make sure you are not experiencing fear and discomfort.

You cling because you are so afraid. It almost feels like a life or death situation. So, you are "clingy". You stay around that person all the time. You do everything that you can to be there for that person all the time.

If you feel like your partner is losing interest that can make you feel immensely afraid. When you feel afraid in this way, you do everything that you can to make sure they do not go away. The way that you do that is by being around them, being in front of them. Trying to get their attention in whatever way that you can.

You feel that your partner or even sometimes non-intimate friends pull away because they often feel overly controlled or observed. This makes you feel even worse and you try even harder, all the while feeling like something is really wrong with you.

You try to control this needy, clingy feeling but you fail because the fear of abandonment wins every time.

~

You feel forgettable and unimportant

You feel unimportant and you feel that people will just leave you and never remember you: it will be as if you never even existed. You believe that you are that unmemorable and unimportant.

You are sure that no one will miss you when you are not with them. You are sure that if some time passes, you would come to mean nothing to them and they will completely forget you as if you never existed. You believe you are forgettable and unimportant.

You imagine that you mean so little, or you mean nothing to anyone at all to the extent that lovers and friends will not ever think about you, you will occupy no space in their mind and heart. They will just walk away because you were never important enough to them. You fear that you are a NOTHING to everyone in every way and you mean nothing to everyone in every way.

~

You feel unworthy of love and not enough as you are

You feel unworthy of love and feel that you are not enough so it is logical to you that no one in your life should stay with you.

You don't feel like anyone could just love you for you so you always have to worry that there are no real, good enough reasons for anyone to stay with you.

~

You are always trying to earn your keep

You always feel like you have to provide some value to be loved or accepted, so you feel like you always have to earn your keep.

That goes for your own love for yourself too. You have to earn your own love as you have to earn everyone else's love.

You have to work hard. You have to be successful. You have to look attractive. You have to be perfect. You always have to provide value for anyone to remain in your life.

...
Once we accept our limits, we go
beyond them.

—*Albert Einstein*

Chapter 3 - Why you have a fear of abandonment

Biological/Genetic memory

We, humans, have a slight tendency to have a fear of abandonment and fear of rejection, and, if given actual evidence for us to hang onto, the fear can be chronic.

There is a generalized fear that our ancestors picked up for survival during the saber-tooth tiger days. Being accepted by others, being a part of a group, and not being rejected by a group gave us a far higher chance of survival.

On the other hand, if you did something the group disapproved of and was rejected and was then of course all alone, you had few ways to defend yourself. You were highly likely to be eaten by some predator.

The humans witnessed the consequences of this and did everything they could to belong to a group so that they would survive. So we have a genetic memory of this even though we no longer have to fear predators who would eat us and end us. This is why we have our general tendencies to have fear of abandonment and fear of rejection from others. This is why we are vulnerable to picking up deep fear from emotional events that happen and have it burrow deep into our psyche that we are easily apt to be abandoned and we have to fear for our lives.

~

If you have a deep fear of abandonment, you have too many times experienced this emotion. This fear of abandonment feels very much as if your very life will end.

~

From now on, I will be covering the more dire, deep burrowed fear of abandonment that you have because you were actually abandoned, physically, or emotionally.

The early experience of abandonment, neglect, and abuse

If you were abandoned at an early age or were neglected or abused, you would have picked up fear that you could not possibly have understood and would have gained a "toxic shame" that you were not good enough, that you do not matter, that you are not important, that you do not have a value.

You would today if you hadn't healed that pain, believe that you are not worthy of love nor enough just as you are.

You may have been left by your parents or a caretaker as a child. You may have lost them through death. You may not have lost them but you may have been abused or neglected.

You may have endured the experience of your parents or guardians going through their own trauma of some kind that destabilized your life as it did theirs.

You may have been brought up by parents or caretakers who were themselves fuelled by a fear of abandonment. The way they related to you and the world around them caused you to feel your world was unstable, insecure, and unreliable.

~

When these painful and scary things were happening to you while you were so little, you were not able to defend yourself. You were not even able to ask or find an expert to ask about the situation.

You did not have knowledge, experience, wisdom, strength, power, or the resources to do any better than to somehow make sense of what was happening to you to your best ability.

~

We throw away what we don't want, so it is easy to gather that you were not wanted.

We usually don't want things that we don't value. So, you would have interpreted that you were not valuable since you were abandoned.

We treat things that we don't value with no care or even badly, crumpling them, breaking them, or throwing them away. As a child, if you are treated badly, beaten, and hurt emotionally and or physically, you adopt the mindset that you are worthless like those things that you would have crumpled, broken, or allowed to break.

The child in those situations, with that kind of treatment, will feel like worthless trash.

You as that little precious child, upon those events happening to you, felt like worthless trash, to be thrown out and forgotten.

~

In the following chapters, I will go over with you just what the effects of this fear have been for your life and what you can do so that you can fully heal yourself and have the amazing life that is waiting for you just on the other side.

...

We are more often frightened than hurt: and we suffer more from imagination than from reality.

-- *Seneca*

Chapter 4 - The effects of a fear of abandonment on your life

Relationship challenges

A fear of abandonment causes the pain and failure of many relationships, intimate ones as well as others. Fear of abandonment does not allow for truly healthy relationships at any level.

In intimate relationships, fear of abandonment makes you live in a state of anxiety, using up all your energy to make sure you do not lose that person. You may give up everything to make sure that the relationship is not lost since losing it feels like death itself. All the while you are conned by your low self-esteem to believe that all that you are doing for that relationship is because you love that person so much.

In fact, when you fear losing that relationship, no matter how much you may actually love that person, you are not able to be your most loving self. This means that you are not able to give the level of love that you could to this person because of your fear of abandonment. This is contrary to what you feel, I know. I remember how it felt to feel so intensely, protecting the possession of that relationship and love of that person. The fear along with love and all that you are trying to manage to keep it all going is a confusing mess disguised in the word "love."

The reason you are not able to give love to the extent that you actually love that person is that the state of being in fear of losing that person — fear of abandonment — causes you to blind yourself, from truly seeing and understanding that person in your life. What that person may experience with you, while you are in a state of fear of losing them, is not feeling loved but needed.

Fear of abandonment also does not allow you to fully enjoy your relationships because it keeps you in a heightened state of critique to try and postpone the abandonment with continual assessments of yourself based on your guesstimation of what right and wrong things are. It can plunge you into spirals of wildly guessing that leave you drained of energy not to mention draining those around you since you are likely to be asking them for answers to your ongoing questions, "Did I do it right? Did I do it wrong?" The fear around those questions only makes others around you feel uneasy, but most importantly it keeps you off-balance and off the emotional solid ground that you are standing on — you just don't know it — if only you could free yourself from those terrible questions.

~

Put up with abusive relationships too easily

Fear of abandonment can also cause you to settle for relationships that offer you far less than love. After an initial honeymoon phase, the awful quality of your object of attraction reveals itself. When this happens you are in such a mode of not losing love, even if it is only the mere idea of love that you initially felt from that person, that you become utterly blind to evaluating the person and the situation.

It is true willful ignorance. You become too preoccupied with your value and worth to that person, even if that person may offer you nothing of any value. Your sole focus is on how you can maintain their love, no matter how little substance exists in this person.

You, in fact, have no idea they are inferior compared to you because you are not looking at them in that context at all. You are too busy looking and questioning your value to them.

In those cases, many people who have a lack of empathy and lack of love for others, like narcissists and opportunists, will grab a hold of you.

They will keep you and use you for their gratification, using you until you are left with nothing for them, and especially for yourself. You become spent and they discard you.

You then feel even more worthless, gaining a deeper fear of abandonment because of the confirmation bias that tells you that you were right to have that fear.

What happens to you next if you do not conquer fear of abandonment is that you are grabbed by the next person who will offer you a mirage of love only to use you yet again, further squeezing the life out of you, the life you are barely holding onto.

You can break this cycle. You must break this cycle now.

~

It affects your ability to love in a healthy way

There is so much that you lose in relation to relationships in your life. We must talk, perhaps most importantly, about our relationships with our children because it is paramount that you conquer your fear of abandonment if you are a parent.

Your fear of abandonment is detrimental to your ability to love your children unconditionally as they need to grow up to be people who can unconditionally love themselves. This will allow them to be authentically happy in their adult lives.

I believe I did this to my child who I love more than life itself. I was steeped in my fear of abandonment while I was bringing him up. I thought I was doing so many great things for him and that I was being a great mom because I was not doing the abusive things that my adoptive parents did to me.

I had also studied a lot about parenting and I was determinedly following all the experts' advice. While focusing on what not to do and following the experts, I was not focused on or was aware of who I was being, which was influenced powerfully by my fear of abandonment.

I would not have admitted it if anyone pointed it out to me out of shame. I did not think that I was that weak. I would have thought of it in those terms: weak. I didn't give myself a chance to really see it.

But while I was a person who lived with this fear underneath all my decisions and all my actions, I feared losing him most of all.

To say that I was overprotective does not even come close to how protective I was. To say that I was needy with him also does not do it justice. I wonder if he felt any pressure from me. The fact that I have no awareness of the degree of how much pressure he must have felt is proof of how selfish I was of needing to feed that fear monster to avoi the pain of being abandoned by the person that I loved and cherished the most.

I wanted him to be strong in all the ways that would lead him to a fulfilling and happy life, but I caused him to become a person who would be codependent like I was when I was in charge of teaching him to live a good life.

I am not condemning myself here, but I am telling you this so that you understand, so that you are warned and so that you can change things for you and your children and not repeat the very mistakes that I made

Holding onto a fear of abandonment is like living right next to a chemical substance that, with continuous exposure, your healthy life has little chance of being realized.

~

Disrupts your life's potential journey

You are always checking over your shoulder to see how you are judged when you carry around a fear of abandonment. You rethink your decisions, you rethink your actions, you rethink just about everything about you to measure yourself against what others might notice is flawed about you because the last thing that you want is to be rejected by anyone in any way

You cannot truly relax. You always have to be vigilant to make sure you are not going to be rejected and abandoned.

Either that or you are forever in a mode of "giving up", you don't ever try to get accepted so that you can just live up to your fear and know that you will always be rejected and unloved and unaccepted, which completely prevents you from getting rejected and abandoned.

People who choose that route in life are often heard saying things like, "I hate people. Everybody just leave me alone." They walk around feeling as if they are the winners of life since they will never lose anything, but truly they lead a miserable life unable to recognize beautiful things even when they are inches away.

There are so many other consequences other than just the intimate relationships for people with a fear of abandonment.

If you have a fear of abandonment, all your relationships are affected by your fear as well. You may find yourself having a hard time getting along in a fulfilling way with just about anyone. Even if you have a lifestyle that surrounds you with a lot of people, you really feel like you have no one that is true in your life.

Fear of abandonment shows up everywhere in your life, in your relationship with people at work, and in other places as well, making you question and feel uncomfortable with any negative signs affecting your working relationships, which then can influence your career.

You have a low self-image

When you fear abandonment, you are accepting a false belief that there's something inferior about you. You may find yourself comparing yourself to others unfairly and disregarding any positives about yourself because your dominant sense is that you are rejectable and unlovable: the very reason why you are apt to be abandoned. Even if something good happens, and you do well at something you are ready to cut short any good feelings.

Since your mind believes you will be abandoned, your logical brain has to agree with you by giving you all the reasons why you are right by having you list all the reasons. This requires you to think the worst about yourself in just about everything and robs you of seeing anything good, even if what is good is extraordinary to every sane person that could see it around you.

Think about those who are anorexic. They see a fat person in the mirror when they are actually unhealthily thin. There are countless talented artists that have come and gone from history who had a crippling fear of abandonment and could not enjoy the brilliant and beautiful work that they created, suffering depression and emptiness, never seeing that so many deeply loved them for who they were.

~

You doubt yourself constantly

You don't deem your decisions trustworthy since you regularly look to see if your decisions are acceptable for others out of fear that your decisions will get you rejected. You cannot genuinely trust the decisions that you make. When others around you are bothered by those aspects of you, you go deeper into self-doubt because others' disappointment with you makes you feel justified in the idea that you are rejectable since it causes inconvenience and disturbs others. You just can't win in your eyes.

In addition, whatever slight annoyance anyone else may feel would likely be blown out of proportion in your mind, judging how they feel about you far more significant than what is taking place in reality.

~

You need others too much

When you have a fear of abandonment, you may need constant feedback that you won't be abandoned, which means you need others to give you the feedback by being there for you at all times.

You might feel rejected when people do not comply with your need for confirmation. You might not realize that you are asking for more than what others may want to give. In addition, when you are in this type of dynamic with anyone, unless they are extremely codependent themselves, they will resent this need and either go away or just not comply. This further deepens your fear that you will be abandoned. You try to rescue yourself from it by stopping those people from not complying or going away. But this, most of the time, exacerbates the rejections leaving you feeling like a victim: abandoned and rejected as you feared.

~

It is difficult to be your best for those who you love

With your fear of abandonment, you will either play the victim or demanding controller. You likely play both. Being a victim of your life and/or being a controller does not allow room for healthy relationships with others. You will often feel victimized or feel stressed out trying to control everything that is occurring between you and those who you love.

It is difficult for you to be at your best for all those who you love because you are unable to be in your best form.

You are not even aware at times, when you are in a profound state of fear, that you are not being your best. You will see it all as if no one is there for you in your time of need and feel abandoned by those who you love instead of seeing that perhaps you are requiring more of them than they can give or handle.

Not being able to see what is truly going on exacerbates the situation. You feel abandoned or not cared for and they, — the people in your life — feel too much is being demanded of them. This leads to a very unhealthy cycle.

...

Fears are educated into us, and can,

if we wish, be educated out.

— Karl Augustus Menninger

Chapter 5 - What you lose if you do not conquer it

I think about how much I have lost in my life because of the fear of abandonment that plagued my existence. My fear of abandonment made me act in ways that hurt those close to me. I can never get those times of safety and closeness back. My fear of abandonment caused me to reject decent and good people from my life because I was beating them to the punch. I feared being rejected so much that I rejected them before they could do it. Looking back I see now that they likely were not going to reject me because of a small incident and if I had been able to sit back and wait, things would have smoothed themselves out in time.

Having a fear of abandonment takes you over and your mind becomes utterly illogical. It is overrun by the monstrous size of fear.

Fear of abandonment caused me to forgo many opportunities for career advancement and even opportunities in my art. I allowed my fear to hold me back because I was too afraid to lose my love of a partner who demanded that I did not pursue my path.

I think about how many years I allowed myself to stay in a painful and abusive relationship because I was afraid to lose that love. I knew intellectually that it was a terrible and unstable relationship with someone who was narcissistic and devoid of empathy who could not and would not do anything for me while demanding that I be there for him in almost every aspect of his needs. I was so desperately unhappy in that relationship and I kept trying to leave but my fear of abandonment kept me frozen with fear and unable to make any progress with my life.

It was painful to be with him but losing him felt like death. That relationship was no life at all and, moment by moment, I felt like I was losing my life to misery.

Still, I stayed utterly confused as to why I was so unable to leave him.

Looking back now, I realize it was that I was so scared of being without him, being without his love, being without a sense of meaning that I felt about myself as long as he loved me and wanted me.

I had some friends who had noticed the change in me while I was with him, that I seemed to become lost and a ghost of my old self. Whatever fight and spirit I had in me before that relationship became buried deep under my fear.

My fear of abandonment has always caused me to make the worst decisions in every important moment of my life. And it definitely kept me from seeing any and all negative intentions from everyone who put me down or discouraged me in any way shape or form. I was losing out on my life. I was losing out on me.

I don't want you to lose time. I want you to not lose out on life, not lose out on you, as I have.

The following are the very important aspects of your life that you do not want to lose out on.

~

True happiness

A fear of abandonment does not make room for your true happiness because it is a domineering thing that keeps you from really seeing things for what they are while you are busy trying to be safe from the bad feelings created by the fear. It is almost impossible to find your true happiness while holding onto this fear.

~

True love

The chances are high that people with a fear of abandonment will be in unhealthy relationships and so losing out on good relationships. So, being able to have true love in your life with a fear of abandonment is difficult unless you are with the most understanding person on earth, who lacks any human insecurities and has a deep sense of confidence and endless source of patience.

It is not easy being a person who has fear of abandonment. It is also not easy being with a person with a fear of abandonment. Can you imagine what it is like for the person who has no idea why their partner is going through all the ups and downs and not able to truly explain all that is going on inside them because they do not know that they are afflicted with fear?

~

True success

With fear of abandonment, it is difficult to have a truly fulfilling life where you experience the best of you.

There are too many things getting in the way of your ability to do that.

If you achieve what others would consider amazing success, you still would not be enjoying it to the fullest possible extent. So, is that a true success? No it isn't.

~

True self-love

When you fear abandonment, you are not loving yourself.

You cannot love yourself while thinking that you have so little worth and so little meaning and so little importance that everyone you love will leave you.

You are not loving yourself as you feel that way about yourself.

It is the lack of self-love that causes you to fear abandonment but it is a fear of abandonment that puts you deeper into the state of devaluing and condemning yourself, making you feel that you are so unworthy of love that you are going to be left behind, rejected, or abandoned.

~

True joy

True joy is robbed from you while you are deep in a fear of abandonment, you are too scared to experience anything joyful.

If joy was right in front of you offering you the gifts of the universe you would not notice joy or the things that would normally cause you joy to the extent that you fully can as long as you have a fear of abandonment inside you.

~

True fulfillment

How do you even pursue true fulfillment when you are standing on the shaky ground of this fear of being abandoned?

How could any sense of fulfillment live in a being who is terrified of being left behind by others? There is no peace in a person who has a fear of abandonment because the fear is so great and scary.

The fear easily takes over and dominates the person so that little else can be experienced by them. The problem is that the person who is going through this does not really know that they are going through it.

They are often only aware of the symptom: the feelings that are caused by a fear of abandonment making it hard to resolve and heal from the real problem.

Fulfillment is far from what a person with a fear of abandonment can achieve.

~

The loss, the price that you pay holding on to this fear, is too high. It only amounts to deep unhappiness and misery. It leads you to miss out on too much.

Being a human being is being in the mode of growth and improvement. Being a human being requires that you continue learning and experiencing more and pushing yourself to stretch.

That means that you, no matter what state you are in, you are to grow and improve yourself, your skills, knowledge, and wisdom.

So why not improve yourself by tackling your fear of abandonment and by doing that not only become happier but act on what you are supposed to do as a human being, grow and self improve? What have you got to lose? What have you got to win?

...

Fear is the main source of superstition, and one of the main sources of cruelty. To conquer fear is the beginning of wisdom.

— *Bertrand Russell*

Chapter 6 - What you gain if you conquer it

Freedom from fear

When you live with a fear of abandonment it is like binding yourself to your own emotional prison inside yourself.

When I used to live with my fear, I didn't even really know that I had a fear of abandonment.

When I would feel it, I used to cover it up with various different excuses.

When I would feel jealous, whether warranted or not, I could not trust my feelings since I was ashamed of feeling jealous. I would either try not to watch and walk away or get angry and have an outburst from having held it in. I used to feel embarrassed and emotionally out of control. I would experience intense fear that felt like a fear of death. It was excruciating.

The contrast with what I feel now is incredible. I now know that I am ok, that I can trust my decisions, that I am solid, that I can decide who I am, and stand on that belief not even wondering what others might be thinking about me. I know that I am ok if someone rejects me, that little of what anyone else does is about me.

I have me and I can rely on myself; I am all that I need. This is actually the very thing that everyone needs. It is the most perfect and optimal way of being.

~

Emotional stability

Fear of abandonment is very powerful and greatly influences our emotional state. It can make us feel out of control, extremely helpless, and deeply and painfully in fear and pain so that we cannot see straight. It can make us lose all sight of logic.

Overcoming a fear of abandonment gives you emotional stability because you don't have the big monster fear machine controlling your emotions and your life.

~

Inner peace

No matter how much wealth and outer success you attain, without inner peace, you have nothing. Without inner peace, you have chaos, drama, sadness, depression, worries, fears, and instability. With inner peace, you have everything because you can see and enjoy life for what life is. You can notice the truth of things because your view is cleared of debris: the unnecessary noise.

~

You know how to love unconditionally (you know how to love in a healthy way without needing them but loving them for them.)

When you are no longer dealing with a fear of abandonment, you now have open space in your heart to love correctly. You will not misconstrue your need for someone as love. You will not be putting undue pressure on those that you love to meet your needs, to appease your needs, but you will have space to really see others for who they are because your vision is free from the blurring effect of a fear of abandonment or fear of rejection. You will know how to love from a solid foundation instead of a shaky foundation.

~

True success

True success is not a lopsided success. True success embodies the wholeness of life: you have outer and inner success. You have prosperity and wealth in the outer and inner world of you. You have a sense of peace about you and everything that you think, feel and do in the outer environment, physical and everything else, where you feel at one and can fully experience inspiration, creativity, spirituality, lightness of being, and oneness of being.

~

True self-love

You will know how to appreciate yourself. In fact, learning to love yourself truly and unconditionally is the key to getting rid of a fear of abandonment.

When you realize that you are whole, and totally and unconditionally worthy of love, when you truly see that, you know that you cannot fear rejection or being left for being unlovable. You stop thinking about that and you are able to live your true life.

~

True joy

You will not have a fear of rejection and a fear of abandonment standing in your way of being able to experience things that bring you joy. You will know how to enjoy the joy because you are in the mode of peace and clarity.

~

True fulfillment

You can experience true fulfillment when you are not constantly focusing on yourself.

If you are constantly under the fear of abandonment, the fear of rejection keeps you focusing on yourself, defending yourself, and worrying about whether you're being left behind or left alone. All of this makes you into a self-centered- person unable to think beyond yourself and see that you are a part of a bigger whole.

When you can rid yourself of a fear of abandonment, you are free to see that you are a part of far more than just yourself and, therefore, you can begin to participate in a life that is far beyond yourself. When you participate in things beyond yourself that is when you find true fulfillment, not before.

...

Of all the liars in the world, sometimes

the worst are our own fears.

– *Rudyard Kipling*

Chapter 7 - Let's begin conquering a fear of abandonment

First: The very first thing that you must do!

Stop all self-blame, shame, embarrassment, negative self-talk, feeling bad about yourself, any and all things that say that something is wrong with you in any way, shape, or form.

Stop all put-downs about your feelings.

Stop all of the self-blame right now.

Stop all of the self-flagellation.

Stop all of the harsh negative self-talk.

Stop all of the "why are you feeling this?"

Next:

Give yourself the courage to be battle-ready!

"I learned that courage was not the absence of fear, but the triumph over it. The brave man is not he who does not feel afraid, but he who conquers that fear"

-- Nelson Mandela

I love that quote by Nelson Mandela. But I am going to go one step further.

Fear is a coward, a paper lion, that wants to survive at all costs.

What I mean by that is that fear has one job. That one job is to help protect us from harm so that we may continue to live.

But fear, when allowed to grow and fester and take over our lives, destroys everything and in the end even undoes the only job it has, which is to help us live by causing us to slowly die.

This means we cannot always trust fear. We must look fear straight in the face to see it for what it is and to not let it overreach and take over our lives.

What I am getting at is this: the very next thing that you must do is adopt a new habit. After stopping all the negative self-condemnation (Step #1), tackle your fear of painful emotions by giving yourself the courage that you need to fight.

And, when you give yourself the courage, tackling your fear of painful emotions is so easy that it will take you only a few tries before you say to yourself, "Oh my, how could I have suffered so much, for so long, when I didn't have to?"

This is what you do. When emotional pain comes on, immediately look directly into that emotional pain and say, "That's ok. It can be there. I am ok."

It is as simple as that. When you say that, you instantly feel a sense of peace. When you say that, you instantly give yourself courage and strength that you didn't know you had. Most importantly, when you say that, you just slammed your opponent — the fear of pain — down on the ground with no effort by just looking straight into its face.

So, the next time you feel emotional pain, any emotional pain, but especially the one that we are talking about in this book — the fear of rejection, the fear of being left behind, the fear of being abandoned — and you are beginning to feel depressed, look straight into the face of that feeling and say, "It's ok, it can be there, I am ok." Watch the bad feelings leave you alone to a feeling of peace.

~

Next: Let's smash the fear of being alone, just for fun, before we move on.

What are some of the fears that you feel when you imagine yourself al alone? ALL ALONE!

Do you feel like it is the end?

Do you feel like you are in trouble in some way?

Do you feel like everyone will reject you?

Do you feel like the ground will disappear beneath you?

Do you feel like everything that you want will just go away?

Do you feel like there is nothing?

Do you feel like you have nothing?

What do you feel?

What are you afraid of?

Why is being abandoned so scary?

Is it being alone? What is it about being alone that is so scary? If you were alone, what would happen then? Why is that so scary? Would you be bored? Would you be in pain? What is the pain? Is it feeling empty? Is it feeling disgusting? Is it feeling ugly? Is it feeling cold? What are you afraid of?

Let's imagine that you were all alone.

What if you were the only one left on Earth? You would be all alone. Your life would not end. You would find a way to survive doing what you can to find joy perhaps in the beauty of nature, creating things that you have the material resources to create for yourself, finding ways to make food so that you can physically survive. You would find a way to be the representative of Earth, the sole member of the human race but still a member of the human race and you would be alive. If there were no predators, you would have nothing at all to fear. You would just exist.

The quality of your life would depend solely on you, what you look at, what you do, how you stimulate your mind, how you spend your time, and how you move through your life.

If you were all alone on Earth, but with access to all things and let's say that there is an energy source there and always will be for some reason.

If you were in such a world you would not be experiencing fear because there is nothing to fear. There is no one. You are all alone. Now, what are you going to do with the rest of your existence? Would you travel the Earth as much as you can to see everything that you can? Would you read all the great books that you can? Would you learn all the musical instruments that you can? Would you learn how to cook all different kinds of food? Would you learn all about genetics to see if you create more humans? Would you learn how to build things? Would you paint to your heart's content?

What would you do with your time?

You would not be afraid.

You would not be afraid since there is no one there for you to fear leaving you.

You would just simply begin LIVING a life.

You would not be living in fear.

~

So, what is the fear in you at the moment?

If you experience a fear of being abandoned, the fear is only significant in your mind. It has become so huge and powerful because it is based on the fear that you experienced when you had no power. It has grown over the years based on the experience that was influenced by your old fear. Fear on top of fear. Fear that helped you grow fear.

~

The fear that you have is not your fault!

You did not volunteer to have a fear of abandonment. You did not volunteer to feel insecure. You did not volunteer to not know that you are worthy of love. You did not volunteer for any of it!!!

Many not only suffer the pain that fear of abandonment causes but also feel bad about themselves while they are feeling it. This only compounds the fear, making you go further into fear's cage. So you have to release all the shame and self-blame. It is the very first and most important step.

Your goal now is to truly conquer this fear of abandonment and live your life exactly the way you want to live it.

~

I want to ask, who would you be if you were not afraid of being abandoned?

Hold that question in your mind and let it just do its work in your subconscious and, with that, let's move on.

Being who you are, or more accurately the actions you are able to take in your life, has been negatively impacted by the fear that has been in your heart. So, if you can go to that imaginary scenario of being completely alone on this Earth, what would you do with your life, with your remaining time on Earth? This is something to keep your thoughts focused on as you move forward and say goodbye to your fear of abandonment.

~

With those things stirring in your mind and taking hold, let's discuss some additional things to consider.

~

Let's take a look at a man who lived most of his life alone. He was not physically alone. He was around people. He was around many people in fact. But, in his emotional life, he was really alone. His name was Marcus Aurelius and he was an emperor of Rome.

Marcus Aurelius was in charge of his people and he took that job very seriously. Because of his level of power and what he expected of himself, his ethics, the morals that he held himself to and since there was no one alive that he could truly rely on for guidance, support or emotional comfort, he lived virtually alone, despite the many subjects surrounding him.

As a release, he wrote in his diary what he must remind himself to do. He confided in his diary the weakness that he must not allow in himself, in his character, through his reminders to himself about how to be the best version of himself for those people who really and truly could not have really seen him for who he was. He should have been lonely.

If needing to be seen, understood, and accepted unconditionally is a human need, Marcus Aurelius must have gone without that for most of his life as an emperor.

As an emperor, especially the kind of emperor that he aspired to be and worked every moment of his life to be, there doesn't seem to have been anyone that matched who he was to even understand him other than the teachers who had come and gone before his time, who were the only ones he seemingly looked to for guidance.

If anyone was emotionally alone on earth, Marcus Aurelius was. Yet he lived a purposeful life of his own making based on his belief that his life really belonged to the whole of the hive: our human race.

He lived his life serving that purpose moment by moment, day by day, year by year, throughout his life.

Marcus Aurelius believed that we are all part of one human race.

He didn't choose this belief not to feel alone nor to make himself feel better about really being alone among many. He believed it and worked to serve the human race, the hive, because that is the mission he accepted when he became an emperor.

With his focus entirely on serving the people for whom he was a guardian, he went to work as one of the bees.

He wrote in his diary that it is impossible to leave one another: "What hurts the hive hurts the bee."

He says things like we are like the "feet, hands and eyes, like that of the rows of teeth, upper and lower," working together to live in cooperation to not only exist but to make this thing called life with one another.

That means that no matter where we dwell physically, we are all connected as a part of one organism.

The fear of being alone is a lie that we adopt.

We are truly alone. And we are truly not alone because we belong to the great human hive.

~

When you look out into a field of mustard flowers, do you imagine that any of those flowers feel afraid of being alone? They do stand alone despite being among many flowers. What you likely think is that those flowers just stand there existing, moving along with life, just being.

We are in some ways the same and, of course, also very different. We are standing among the fields of all kinds of flowers. We can just be. Unlike the flowers, we are luckily able to move among ourselves affecting our field/world with more free will, power, and creativity. We have so many more aspects of ourselves at our disposal, being human beings.

So, with far more power, clearly far more power than the beautiful mustard flower, but with no fear in our own existence like the mustard flower, we can move through our world physically or spiritually, making our impact, making our beautiful brushstrokes.

~

Stoics, like Marcus Aurelius, taught that we must focus on those things that we have control over, leaving behind those things that we do not have control over.

What you do not have control over is what took place in your past that has hurt you, what has caused you pain and suffering and in the end the fear of abandonment that has impacted your life in the ways that are causing you further pain in your life now.

What you do not have control over is what has taken place already. What you do not have is control over is knowing the exact reasons why. What you do not have control over is getting apologies for the wrongs that a person, group of people, or simply misfortune has dealt to you and your loved ones.

When you put energy into anything that you do not have control over, you further your suffering, stunt your growth, rob yourself of true success and happiness, and even impact your health.

~

So, now let's focus on what you do have control over.

You have control over what you focus on. You have control over the actions that you take. You have control over the decisions that you make, which will affect how the actions that you take turn out. So, what does that mean for conquering a fear of abandonment?

Let's imagine that you are the general of an army. How do you win a battle? Do you win a battle when you fear your enemy? When you keep your focus on all the reasons why you should be afraid of your enemy, can you win the battle no matter how strong and fortified your army is?

~

George B. McClellan was a general in the Union Army fighting for the North during the American Civil War. He was good at training and building his army but no matter how well-trained his army was and how much larger his army than his enemy's, he lost battles causing casualties that he could have prevented because he was afraid of his enemy and could not make up his mind to take action and when he did act, he made timid, small moves that lost him the lives of his men and his battles. He did this again and again, never really learning his lessons and, in the end, living out his life jealous toward a general who took the opposite strategy and won battles over and over again.

~

The general that McClellan was so jealous of was Ulysses S. Grant, born Ulysses Hiram Grant.

He trained his men. He fortified his men. He used his intelligence to come up with innovative, creative, and intelligent battle strategies. But what made him the complete opposite of McClellan was that he did not focus on what may be scary about his enemy but focused on what he must do to "whip" his enemies.

Though he did lose a few times, he not only won far more battles than McClellan but all other union generals during his time, he went on to win the war and save his nation from not only separation from itself but also from further war and so further deaths.

~

So, what does this mean for you? It means that you can do what Gran did and focus on your tasks at hand. Your goal is to conquer your enemy. Your enemy. Your enemy is the fear of abandonment.

The first step in beating your enemy is facing it. Facing the fear of abandonment is deciding that you are going to beat it no matter what it takes.

That is your only choice if you want to be free of it. That is your only choice if you want to know true joy. That is your only choice if you want to not only know love for yourself but also know how to truly love another because without it your love for others will be hindered. Your only choice is to decide to free yourself from what has shackled you for far too long. You deserve to free yourself. You deserve to be free!

~

With your new winning paradigm, let's now talk about some techniques.

When you run into the emotions produced by your fear of abandonment, be your very own attorney as well as your own general who takes action to win battles.

When fears come up, give yourself an argument based on logic. Have a debate where you make points and counterpoints against what you are feeling and question why you are feeling the feelings.

Offer yourself an argument to counter the beliefs behind your fears. Talk with yourself logically. Keep practicing talking to yourself logically.

Create phrases to counter your beliefs about the fear and say them. For example: "That's ok. You can be there, feeling. I can handle this feeling., etc."

Then as the general of your army, take actions that counter your fear and see that nothing bad happens. For example, if you are afraid that your spouse will leave you if you leave them alone or do something for yourself or make a decision to do something like take a class or get into music, etc, if you are afraid of those things or any other benign things, do them and watch how they do not leave you.

Challenge your fears by doing what you are afraid to do because of your fears (nothing dangerous or immoral and unethical, of course).

Keep taking those actions following your logic but not your irrational fear.

Experiencing the opposite of your fears will also help you to unlearn your fear of abandonment.

Learn how to love yourself

This is perhaps the most important thing. The fear of abandonment actually puts importance on what you do not need and what you do no have any control over. Someone else loving you or staying with you forever is completely out of your control. Therefore, depending on it, counting on it, and focusing on it is futile. You can love another and enjoy being loved back. That really is all that is true and real. You cannot control another person and you cannot control life.

You can control yourself. And, in truth, it is your self-love that not only do you have full control over but is the very thing that you need above all else so that you can function to your full potential: fully good, fully loving, fully giving, fully making a positive difference in this world.

If you don't love yourself, no matter how many people love you and stay with you to the end, you will continue to feel empty and lonely. You will not only not know how to fully enjoy the love of others, because you will not be able to recognize it, but you will doubt it and distrust it. In fact, you will not trust those who love you because you cannot see why they love you when you don't love you. Therefore, the fear of abandonment and the fear of rejection will go on thriving in your misery.

Pursue your passion

Pursuing your passion is an act of self-love. I am talking about something that you truly, truly, truly believe in. I feel I need to say it that way because it is not always easy, especially for those who are in the habit of not feeling worthy or are worried incessantly about what others think and fear rejection, to pursue what they want in their lives. You may not be and likely are not in the practice of taking yourself seriously so even if what you truly believe in is staring at you inches away from your eyes, you may not recognize it. You may have judged it as unimportant or silly.

You may be thinking that you are not important, not good enough, not smart enough, not capable enough, not clever enough, not intelligent enough, not important enough, not wealthy enough, not attractive enough, not fit enough, not skilled enough, not experienced enough... There are so many more "not enough" beliefs, all of them preventing you from taking action toward what you truly believe in.

By contrasting that self-doubt with your actions, even if you just cannot imagine that you can do it now, by taking actions toward acting on what you truly believe in, your mind will catch up with your actions when it sees the result of your actions. It is the most amazing experience to see a different, greater side of you, greater because you are taking actions to manifest things that you thought were out of your reach.

When you act on your true beliefs and continue to pursue them, even i
you see no results for a while, just even if you're starting it, taking
actions will start to change you and change your beliefs about yourself
The feelings that you have when you are working on what is true for
you force you to grow into yourself, the person that you were
supposed to be, the person that you were meant to be, what is written
in your DNA.

And, as you live into it, grow into the size that you were supposed to
be, you will begin to feel the whole of you, the you that is real, and the
you that is there for you. You will begin to know how to take yourself
your ideas, your inspirations, who you are seriously. You had always
needed you, the whole you, nothing but the whole you, and you are
just discovering it. That is the truth of everything.

~

Transcend

As you pursue the real truth, which is that you need to be self-reliant,
to love yourself, to lead yourself, to create yourself, to manifest
yourself, to motivate yourself, to guide yourself, to realize yourself,
you then see that you are here to take part in the greater whole.

Your true potential will only be freed upon fully realizing yourself, at
which point you are fully equipped to participate in the growth of a
peaceful and whole universe.

You do this by doing fulfilling work, work that helps your fellow human beings.

You are now helping as a whole person, not as a person who relies on others' approval. You are helping others from a place of wholeness which means that you are truly helping others in a healthy way.

By pushing, stretching, and meeting your truest potential, you complete the process of becoming your whole person.

...

Do the thing you fear and the death

of fear is certain.

— *Ralph Waldo Emerson*

Chapter 8 - Let's cement the conquest by building supportive habits and mindsets

The following things are your life's foundations that establish, build, and strengthen you as a person to enable your growth and healing.

In addition, by following these habit-building activities and steps, you organically heal emotional wounds inside you as well as gaining a positive and clearer view of yourself which then gives you the insights and knowledge to clear away the false stories about yourself that you have adopted in your mind and heart.

Though the following may sound mundane, they are essential and crucial things to add to your life. Make them a permanent fixture in winning the battle over your fear of abandonment.

~

Establish and practice an excellent self-care routine every day.

Self-care is very important. It offers a solid foundation you can build on to be free to be your best, feel your best, think your best, learn your best, and experience life to the fullest.

~

Alcohol

To heal the emotional wounds of your childhood, to re-examine the stories that you have adopted, to re-evaluate who you are and what you are worth and the true reasons for all that took place, to do all of that with your mind, you must be in an optimal physical condition so that your body can allow the learning and understanding to take place. Reaching for your higher and best self is greatly helped when you allow yourself to be free of substances that can make you experience emotional ups and downs like alcohol.

Alcohol zaps away dopamine and serotonin from your brain, so the next day your brain lacks what you need to be as happy as possible.

Alcohol can make you feel depressed as it is a depressant. It is difficult to know exactly what it is that you are experiencing: actual depression or physical alcohol-based depression.

If you are in that state on a regular basis, it colors your experience with your life without you truly knowing where your feelings are coming from.

With your commitment to truly heal your whole self, you can give yourself a gift of powerful healing by keeping your mind, body, and spirit in their best mode by giving yourself a break from alcohol.

~

Exercise

The benefits of exercise are indisputable. There is really and truly nothing else that compares with the amount of benefits that exercise gives. It helps us pursue just about every goal related to healing and growing the physical and emotional aspects of ourselves.

Doing it first thing in the morning is the easiest to implement as well as giving you continuous benefits throughout your day.

Once it becomes a habit, exercise takes little to no self-control or discipline to do it. It becomes a mindless act, and, if you are doing something positive mindlessly and effortlessly, you are fortunate.

Next, the benefit of exercising first thing in the morning is that the positive effects of exercise on your brain and your body will last throughout your day. It is like taking a timed release feel-good vitamin that aids you throughout the day.

You will also, contrary to what you might think, feel more energetic throughout your day, having exerted yourself in the morning. I had always wondered why I felt stronger and more energetic when I exercised in the morning compared to when I didn't. I thought it was all in my head. Research now shows that you are able to be more active throughout the day when you've done your exercise in the morning.

If you are not exercising regularly or have not been doing it for a while, you can start by doing 5 minutes of something in the morning. Tell yourself your only obligation is to get up and do 5 minutes but do it every day at the same time.

Soon, your body will naturally want to do more. Listen to your desire to do more and add more time to your workout as you go. If what you are doing is aerobics, you can add short intervals of strength training: sit-ups, push-ups, light weights, etc.

You will sweat and feel the benefit of endorphins in your brain. The endorphins will give you a sense of well-being and emotional strength to tackle what you want to address. Because you will start your day by doing it, your whole day will be affected by your morning boost, and you will feel more energized and your mind will be clearer. You will also walk taller, feeling the strengthening of the muscles in your body, which is a reminder of your power and ability to heal. You will feel agile and strong. And, of course, the added and fantastic benefit of this is that your health improves, and a sense of vitality is a tremendous gift to give yourself every day.

The thing about investing your energy into your body's health is that the energy investment comes back to you instantly and daily, giving you back the energy that you need to live the joyful and fulfilling life that you deserve. Exercise is one of your very best friends during this time of healing. And it will remain one of your very best friends long after.

~

Getting quality sleep

During most of my adulthood, I have sacrificed sleep, motivated by my desire to maximize productivity. I kept my body full of caffeine and sugar and dealt with regular fatigue, sleepiness, erratic moods, low energy, and a less-than-desired level of focus in my work and learning.

Once I began to learn about the importance of sleep in health and even productivity itself, my brain understood it and accepted it, but I still refrained from using my knowledge. Now that I fully practice it, I cannot talk enough about how it has positively affected my emotional balance, energy, memory, sense of well-being, happiness, and, in fact, my productivity and mental focus.

~

Eat foods that heal and feed your body and mind.

Mindfully eating foods that elevate your mood instead of detracting from your spirits is a good way to nurture your well-being and lovingly and consciously take good care of your body. You want to give yourself as much mental strength and emotional power to process your fear and allow your natural mind to do its work to find answers and learn things about yourself by eating foods that give you mental and physical strength.

Foods I find helpful are fish, chicken, and lots of green vegetables while completely staying away from refined sugar and refined carbs. You want to eat foods that keep your moods even and stable as much as possible so that you can think as well as possible in stressful circumstances. Omega 3, 6, and 9 in flaxseed oil, multivitamins, and going outside for sun exposure are also very helpful.

~

Keep your body hydrated.

Keeping hydrated is not just good for your physical health but also for mental health. Research shows that being dehydrated can cause moodiness and even feelings of depression. We all have been advised by health experts about the importance of hydration but the effect of hydration on our emotional wellbeing is not a popular knowledge. The power water has on our moods is immense. Therefore, keeping your body hydrated is not just a key part of the healing journey but also beneficial for your daily routine.

~

Meditation

Daily meditation helps you learn how to be in the moment. When you are in the present moment it is easy to see that life is OK, that life is not falling in on you, you are not losing anything, etc. Meditation helps you to organically unlearn irrational feelings of fear, making us, over time, become more emotionally balanced and self-reliant.

Over time you began to experience yourself in ways that you may have never felt yourself: the energy of you, the essence of you, the whole of you. You feel the warm joy and glow of just being. You feel quiet, peaceful empowerment within yourself.

When you meditate you are in the present moment and you are embodying your whole self, you see that you are whole. You have no missing piece. There is no abandonment. You are here. You are.

Focus and develop your life

Developing your life is essential and immeasurably powerful in helping you to gain an appreciation of your value while losing the fear of abandonment and fear of rejection.

People who have a fear of abandonment have come to rely on what others think of them to experience any amount of happiness. One of the most practical, useful, and efficient ways to become fearless is by facing your fear head-on and fearlessly doing your own thing, disregarding others who may judge you. When you take such bold actions and focus on developing your OWN life, you teach yourself in an instant that there is nothing to fear. YOU are who you can and must come to rely on to move forward into YOUR life.

~

Self-love

You gained a fear of abandonment through the experience of actual abandonment or a prolonged slow abandonment of neglect and unstable or unreliable love and attention.

To undo that effect in the long run and also to support what you are learning in terms of becoming free of this fear of abandonment, to crush it, incorporate a regular practice of self-love so that you can learn that you are worthy of love.

~

Knowing how to love yourself is actually as simple and easy to learn as it is important to learn. By learning how to love yourself and practicing loving yourself, you learn that you are worthy of love. And when you learn and know that you are worthy of love, you learn that you are not abandonable and that you are not a candidate for abandonment. You no longer need to fear being abandoned.

Since love is action, and since you were not loved through actions or you were rejected through actions, what you have to do is to simply take loving actions to love yourself.

The first loving action you must begin doing is practicing lovingly and mindfully tending to your wants and needs.

What do loving parents do? They do their very best to meet their child's needs and they pay attention lovingly and mindfully to the things that their child wants. Loving parents know that meeting their child's needs is essential. A loving parent lovingly listens to their child's wants and mindfully takes action by giving them things and experiences that are good for them, which will give them true joy while keeping at bay things that they want that are not good for them.

In the way that a loving parent tends to the wants and needs of a child that they love, you can now lovingly and mindfully tend to your wants and needs which will give you the experience of being loved. By meeting those needs and wants you are showing yourself and teaching yourself that you are lovable and you are worthy of love.

If you continue to ignore your wants and needs, you are going to continue to believe that you are not worthy of love, you are not valuable, and you are not important to you.

If you were chronically neglected as a child, if that is the childhood that you had, you are well accustomed to ignoring your needs and wants. The problem with that is that ignoring your wants and needs is withholding love and affirming to yourself that the lie that you accepted as a child has validity. Ignoring your wants and needs now makes you feel just as unloved as it made you feel when you were only a child. You felt unlovable then and you feel unlovable now.

You now have the power to change all that. It is time to start paying attention and taking loving actions for yourself.

What do you enjoy eating? What do you enjoy doing? What music do you like listening to? What kinds of conversations do you enjoy having? Where do you like spending your time? What kind of people do you feel happy being around? What color do you feel happy being around? What flowers do you like having around? What values do you feel strongly about?

Be mindful of your wants and needs and tend to them as if you are your own loving, kind, and generous parent. As you practice this moment by moment, hour by hour, day by day, watch yourself start to stand up straight, own the space where you live as a person who belongs, not to the group that you see in front of you necessarily, but to the Universe in which you live. You are here. You are worthy of love.

~

The next loving action you must take is to fall in love with your flaws. Brene Brown, the author of *Daring Greatly* and many other amazing books, says that a true friend or your true tribe loves you not in spite of your flaws but because of your flaws. If your best friend loves you for your flaws, shouldn't you love you at least as much as your best friend does?

The flaws that I am talking about are aspects of yourself that you have come to believe are imperfections. They are things that you have no power to change and you feel less than good about yourself when attention is called to them, and, in fact, your feelings about that aspect of you or those aspects of you quietly chip away at your sense of self-value.

Are you too tall, too short, too full-figured, or too skinny? Do you have big feet, small feet, a big nose, or a small nose? You likely believe something about you is not up to par or makes you less than lovable.

The thing is, hating any part of you that you were born with is a waste of your time and energy. Hating them does nothing good and only causes harm to your sense of self. Your only choice is to fall madly in love with them. It is absolutely possible to love something that you have hated.

Remember how you felt about an aspect of a person whom you fell in love with. Aspects of them that you may have found annoying and deeply unattractive suddenly became the most adorable and loveable parts because those parts belonged to the person whom you were deeply in love with.

When you are in love with someone, you love everything and anything about them unconditionally. Shouldn't you love yourself in the same way? It is that simple. Just give yourself love the way you love the person you are in love with. Take a look at the part or parts of you that you have hated, and look at them with loving eyes, as if you are your loving parent loving those parts of you because those parts belong to a person who you love. Feel the same love for those aspects of you.

~

Another loving action to practice is trusting yourself enough to take chances on yourself. If you grew up being bullied into submission and made to feel you weren't worth much with statements like "Who do you think you are?", you may be accustomed to never risking failure nor attempting to succeed. Things that you want so badly may just seem far too big for your britches.

Pushing yourself to take a big chance and doing the very thing that you don't think that you can is a huge loving act that you must practice doing daily.

~

Practicing self-kindness is another important loving action. When someone makes a mistake, it gives you a chance to practice patience and kindness. Even if you are in a position to be teaching them or guiding them, the best way to do it is with patience and kindness. No matter the situation, patience and kindness always go a long way to bringing about the best outcome.

Many of us put effort into following that principle; even if we are not always successful, we at least try to do it and if we fail at being kind we feel bad about it. When it comes to our own mistakes and failures or even something that has gone wrong that we're not the cause of, we find ourselves being the complete opposite of kind toward ourselves. In fact, most of the time we are not even aware that we should be kind to ourselves and we don't even regret not having been kind to ourselves like we would regret it if we had been less than kind to someone else.

We need to become more deeply aware of needing to be kind to ourselves and in fact when we take the loving action of being mindful and kind to ourselves at all times, we will automatically know how to be kind to others in stressful situations when something goes wrong or when there is a failure or mistake of some kind.

It is a powerful way to love yourself and gives you a deeper ability to love others.

Practicing self-kindness means you hold feelings of kindness toward yourself even during moments when you find yourself feeling at fault. This means that you have a general sense of love toward yourself no matter what the momentary condition might be. This means that you hold in your heart feelings of unconditional gentleness, patience, peace, and love toward yourself.

Can you imagine what kind of a person you would be to everyone around yourself when you are practicing self-kindness at all times? Can you imagine what kind of energy you would be putting out to the world, to your universe, as you take measures to be kind and gentle to yourself always? You are making a positive difference to the whole world by cultivating this kindness toward yourself. This practice is a must when you are practicing self-love.

~

The next important loving action is practicing self-compassion on your path to loving yourself. Most of us are far too hard on ourselves over the littlest of things, thinking that perhaps we may do better or that we somehow deserve the harshness because that's what we received as children.

Practicing self-compassion during times of stress, pain, and challenge only helps us to be our best. We are then free of the heavy debris of harsh self-messages. We are creating emotional peace to think through things rationally, problem-solving, feeling necessary emotions, and able to perform tasks in the best possible way.

We don't lose a thing with self-compassion but we do lose greatly when we do the opposite. The harshness toward ourselves that lacks self-love costs us a sense of peace, the ability to think well, and the drive to perform our best with what we need to tackle or create.

There is only one good choice if we want to live our best life and that is to practice self-compassion at all times.

~

Another important loving action is providing ourselves with joyful experiences. Does watching the waves of the ocean bring you joy? Do flowers? Does painting a picture or taking a photo give you joy? Does having coffee with a good friend give you joy? Does a deep conversation with your best friend give you joy? Does getting a massage gives you joy? Does singing give you joy? Whatever it is that gives you joy, appreciation for beauty, and the gratefulness to be alive fuels your life and puts you on a vibrant path to help you be your best. It means you are being the best version of yourself.

~

Another loving action is protecting your time. Be mindful of how you spend it. Say "yes" only to things that are meaningful and fulfilling to you.

Avoid toxic people and toxic situations. They drain your energy, passion, and your ability to experience your flow. Toxic people and toxic situations prevent everything good that you have the right to experience in your life. It is a waste of your precious time.

Don't kill time ever! If you have to wait with nothing to do, you can listen to an audiobook that inspires you and focuses you on your life path. Journal. Use, spend and invest every moment of your time. Remember the things that you value and let the time that you spend reflect the things that you value.

Grow your belief that you are enough and you are worthy of love by retelling your old negative stories.

Take opportunities to retell your stories when you feel bad about yourself.

Whenever you feel bad, depressed, anxiety, etc., the root of those negative feelings most often comes from saying something harsh, derogatory, and negative toward yourself about yourself. Sometimes if you are lucky, you know exactly what you said. However, sometimes, you have no idea that you said these horrible things about yourself because what you said to yourself was far beyond words that your mind could easily detect. It was a belief that started with words that have turned into a feeling and shot directly to your mind and heart before you could even argue using facts, the truth, or a logical assessment of yourself.

If you are often depressed and in a negative mood all the time, you are likely being constantly bombarded with these emotions that had long ago established themselves with false words. They are now just your regular daily routine being shot at you anytime a potential trigger is presented in front of you.

So now what you will have to do is to become the Sam Spade of your own story, or if you prefer the British version, Sherlock Holmes or Miss Marple.

Here is what you do.

First, keep in the back of your mind to never waste a bad moment or bad feeling on depression or anxiety.

When you feel any negative emotions, take out your journal. If you are driving, do it in your mind and think about your discovery in the order that your thoughts processed the emotions all the way to the end the new answer, the new story, the new emotions about it. If you can please pull your car over to a safe place, and, if you are not driving, again, take your journal, and began to write down the questions then the answers to the following:

- First, ask yourself what took place just before your negative emotion appeared in yourself. Write down the answer.

- Next, ask yourself what it was about that answer that made you feel bad or what the meaning of that answer is. Write down the meaning that you applied to that incident.

- Next, ask yourself, where you got that meaning, who taught you that that meaning applied to you in the way that you believe it does. Write down the names of people or a person who repeatedly told you that message.

- Then, review, from your adult's mind, with all the understanding that you have of humanity and especially children, ask yourself, if you agree with that assessment of who you were. Look at your childhood self from yourself today and look at the person or people who told you those things. What do you think of them? What kind of people were they? Were they right about most things? Then, view yourself and assess who you are from your own perspective (if this is hard for you, assess yourself from the most loving, wise, and the kind famous person that you know and see your childhood self from that person's perspective.) Write down all the answers in the order of the questions listed.

- What was your answer to you, or, if you don't know, what was the assessment of you from the eyes of the most loving, kind, and wise person that you know? What was the assessment of you? Was that child, you, a child who is worthy of love, good and innocent... a child?

- I don't even know you, but I know that you were worthy of love, good and innocent. You were a child like any other child. You were worthy of love.

I will give you an example from my own exercise that I did to affirm your understanding of what you need to do to gain the truth about the old messages that you have bought hook, line, and sinker, and how you can move into the new and logical messages that you must now adopt so that you can live your powerful truth.

On July 4th, 2017, I was standing in my backyard deck with my coffee in hand and could hear clearly the happy music from the park a few blocks away. The celebration was in the air. People were out to take in that air but I wanted nothing to do with it.

I was just fresh from a break-up and wasn't even at a point of trying to heal. I was barely keeping on top of the pain of the heartbreak.

When the brass music began to play, I sunk into the horrible abyss of dark feelings and I could not keep pain at bay any longer. I was feeling it. It hurt. I felt depressed.

There was an emotional police officer standing by metaphorically but she was standing by. That police officer was what I had implemented in my life during those days.

I had begun to investigate my pain and journal everything that I was experiencing and learning with an aim to cure my inability to love myself.

So I began asking my questions.

- What just happened before I felt depressed? My answer: The brass band played. My ex is a brass band musician and if he and I were still together I would be at an event like it with him.

- What made me feel bad? My answer: I am not with him.

- Why does that make me feel bad? My answer: He has rejected me and he does not love me anymore.

- What does it mean about you, if he doesn't love you anymore? My answer: I am not loveable.

- Does him not loving you anymore, does that actually make you not lovable? My answer: I don't know. I guess not.

- Was there someone in your childhood that told you that you are not lovable? My answer: Yes, my adoptive parents. They told me repeatedly and often.

- What kind of people were they? My answer: They were both narcissistic, self-centered, unhappy and confused people.

- Can you rely on them to be right about their assessment of people? My answer: No.

- Can you rely on their assessment of you? My answer: No.

- Take a minute or more and as if you are time traveling, go there to that time when you were a little girl and look at that girl: what do you see? My answer: I see a girl who is without support, all alone. Yet, I see a strong, innovative, smart, creative, thoughtful girl who always came up with fun things to do for her friends. I don't see an ugly girl or a bad girl or an unlovable girl. If she was mine, if she was my daughter, I would adore her and find her so much fun to watch growing up.

- Take a minute to tell her how you are feeling right now, tell her who you see in her and tell her what she will be doing in her future. My answer: I am so sorry that you are having to live in so much fear and pain. You don't deserve that and you should not have been going through that. You are so cute and you are really a good girl. I want you to know that you are going to overcome all that you are going through and by overcoming it, you are going to be able to help a lot of people who are in pain. You are going to do beautiful things because of the pain that you are going through right now. I love you.

I actually went through those steps that I just showed you. Doing that has had a profound effect on my healing. It is very important and powerful that you do that as many times as you can to flush out the false story and establish the true, rational story about yourself.

If you still are not clear about what to do, please contact me via my website and send me your questions:

www.healyourheartandfindyourlife.com

...

You teach best what you most need to

learn.

-- Richard Bach

Chapter 9 - Teach others, help others and deepen your healing

Changing your mindset, shifting your paradigm, and healing your heart is amazing and wonderful.

Having the changes, shifts, and healing continue for you is essential so it can become permanent.

It is not just about permanency but also encouraging further growth and expansion because there is always ample room for more growth and expansion in yourself.

Just imagine how you would feel to see yourself involuntarily learn and shift more and more and more, months from now, six months from now, a year from now, on and on.

That is exactly what has happened for me and still happens to me, now even more powerfully in some ways.

It never surprises how many dividends are paid to me from that two months period when I devoted myself to changing all my fears and insecurities.

One aspect that boosts my growth is that I am dedicated to helping others learn what I have. I want everyone to have what I have.

The healing that has taken place in me is simply amazing.

I want that for you, hence, I am asking you to help others learn and heal from their fear of abandonment.

Take your own healing and help others to heal as you are healing from this book and, when you do that, there is no way you can go back to being dominated by fear, any fear.

~

When you actively help others, you will feel inspired as you inspire others to grow and heal deeper and deeper. You will get better and better every time.

...

Who sees all beings in his own self, and his own self in all beings, loses all fear.

— Isa Upanishad, Hindu Scripture

Chapter 10 - What your conquering of this fear means for the world

You will spread authentic positivity in the following ways:

You will be empowered and happy. You will hold that kind of energy toward all whom you relate to, intimate and otherwise.

When you are a person who has lost the fear that has drained you for so long and you no longer have that load, you will have so much more positive energy in your life. You will be creating in ways that you have not been before. You will be your original voice in ways that you have not before. You will be adding not only positivity but your own

unique voice, messages, and beauty to the world in ways that you hav
never done before.

~

As a unique and self-trusting voice, you will have the wisdom to help
others to learn, which adds to the growth and healing of our world.

You will inspire true and honest communication because you will be
communicating like that with everyone that you come across.

Without fear of abandonment, you can speak your mind. You will
become more authentically confident or comfortable about speaking
about things that are real to you. You are not editing yourself and you
will become more comfortable with your own thoughts and the persor
who you actually are.

~

You will also become more in touch with your true feelings. You will
also come to believe in your feelings and your thoughts in ways that
you had not felt before because you are not afraid of being rejected fo
your thoughts and feelings. As you express yourself honestly and
courageously, you inspire those around you to do the same.

~

You will be a self-empowered person, able to love and empower
others, just what our world desperately needs from us.

As the best and strongest version of you, you are more empowered than before to take actions that truly make a difference in our world. Knowing how to truly love is an art of true healing for you and for everyone around you. When you actually know how to love, not out of need or a place of fear, but actually seeing others for who they are, knowing how to unconditionally love, unconditionally accept, and unconditionally be curious — instead of just needing love and acceptance from them —you will inspire others to do the same and your love will be felt by those around you in an authentic way. That is healing.

~

You will be more in alignment with your true self. That means you will make choices and act on things that are truest to you, which, in turn, makes you participate in the health and true beauty of our world. This energy is so needed in our world that can sometimes be ruled by unqualified-less-than-wise-people who spread distrust, creating a world that is dysfunctional and fuelling inequality. You will be doing the opposite. You will inspire trust and stability.

~

You will be fearless in the things that you do. Your being fearless will inspire others to be fearless. You will truly take flight into the lightness of you, the joy of you, the fullness of you. You will effortlessly take part in changing our world for the better just by being you.

About the Author

Nancy Sungyun grew up a California girl. At sixteen, she dove into a life of learning to master her emotional self. Her curiosity about learning theory led her to a master's degree in education at the University of Southern California. Her aspiration to guide others to healing led her to three years of life coach training from CoachU university, founded by Thomas Leanord.

Nancy coaches her clients on their journey to master the key emotional skills so that they can find their very best lives.

You can find out more about Nancy's work at

www.healyourheartandfindyourlife.com

https://www.youtube.com/c/nancysungyun

Made in United States
North Haven, CT
23 December 2023

46509474R10098